C E N T E N N I A L   P R E S S

BLUFF YOUR WAY IN OFFICE POLITICS

Joseph T. Straub

CENTENNIAL PRESS

ISBN 0-8220-2217-6
Copyright © 1990 by Centennial Press

Printed in U.S.A.
All Rights Reserved

Centennial Press, Box 82087, Lincoln, Nebraska 68501
an imprint of Cliffs Notes, Inc.

MEMORANDUM

To: Aspiring Bluffer
From: Bluffer's Guide Central
Subject: Office Politics

No matter how much you know about business, the odds are that you haven't read a single book about office politics. In fact, this is probably the only book you've seen that even *mentions* the subject, right? And, because it holds the key to your business success (not to mention the welfare of your spouse, assorted children, and miscellaneous household pets that you'll own during the next forty years), you should run to the checkout counter and buy it immediately. Go ahead. We'll wait.

Now then: Many of the books you've studied in high school or college no doubt had the word "Principles" in their titles. You won't find one titled *Principles of Office Politics*, though. Why not? Because there *aren't* any principles in office politics! Scheming, manipulating, and maneuvering, yeah. Principles? Nah! But never fear. With us under your arm (we hope you used deodorant this morning), we'll explore some business realities together.

Books about office politics are so rare because people feel uncomfortable talking about the subject. It ranks right up there with hemorrhoids, bad breath, yeast infections, armpit hair, and the heartbreak of psoriasis. Most companies don't like to admit that they have a political side, and those that will don't have any suggestions about how to deal with it. That's where this book gives you a competitive edge.

Think of it as a bed. You can have lots of fun and gain plenty of wisdom between the covers. Relate it to your job (this book, not your bed), and you'll acquire the three Ps of success (power, prestige, and promotions) much faster than your coworkers, all of whom, you may believe, should be poster children for birth control.

Congratulations on your practicality and sense of self-preservation. If you have the time, let us know how things work out. We'll do lunch. Your treat.

SOME WORDS OF WISDOM FOR OFFICE POLITICIANS

"I yield to no one in my admiration for the office as a social center, but it's no place actually to get any work done."
Katharine Whitehorn

"The modern corporation is a political institution; its purpose is the creation of legitimate power in the industrial sphere."
Peter Drucker

"Practical politics consists in ignoring facts."
Henry Adams

"Those who act as if they know more than their boss seldom do. Those who do, have sense enough not to make it obvious—to the boss."
Malcolm Forbes

"Next to knowing when to seize an opportunity, the most important thing in life is to know when to forgo an advantage."
Disraeli

"Trust everybody, but cut the cards."
Finley Peter Dunne

"When in danger or in doubt, run in circles, yell and shout."
Dr. Laurence J. Peter

A HISTORY OF
OFFICE POLITICS

Office politics have been around as long as offices. Longer, in fact. Like as far back as prehistoric times, when Mogluk the Neanderthal, the first of his band of happy campers to stumble on a cave, went to the rear and built a fire. No Rhodes scholar, he. Gorp, the last member to enter, built his fire near the door. The wind kicked up and blew smoke from Gorp's fire to the back of the cave, were it almost asphyxiated Mogluk. Mogluk said something unprintable (because printing hadn't been invented yet), lumbered to the front of the cave, went upside Gorp's head with a mammoth's shinbone, and took over his fire. Gorp, feeling miffed and suffering from a slight concussion, scuttled to the rear of the cave, where necessity forced him to invent the respirator and oxygen tent. He later started a successful medical equipment company.

Now let's fast-forward to today's corporate office, which has a lot in common with a cave, except for carpeting and central heat and air. What makes them so much alike? The same jockeying for position! Yes, competition is alive and kicking butt in today's corporations. Things are more technologically advanced, of course (you can use political clout instead of a mammoth's shinbone to persuade your colleagues), but the age-old concepts of territorial imperative and one-upmanship hang in there like rusty fishooks.

In today's large companies, for example, peons whose desks are clustered in the middle of the floor plot to maneuver themselves into cubicles. Members of the cubicle clan are hellbent on maneuvering themselves into four-walled offices. Four-walled office residents are pulling strings to get *corner* offices, where they belatedly realize they're vulnerable to attacks from two directions instead of just one. Ah, the price of success.

Some companies have such a huge number of lower-level employees that your typical department resembles a huddled mass of neatly dressed clones (which management patronizingly calls "associates") awaiting processing through a surrealistic corporate Ellis Island. In these companies, people give you directions to their desks by citing the number of the nearest pillar. (Stop that, we're serious!) If you have to see someone you've only talked to on the phone, he says something like "I'm the eighth desk south of G-3." This sounds ludi-crous—like he's calling in an air strike to keep his posi-tion from being overrun. Anyone in these firms who's foolish enough to wander around without a map and compass may never be heard from again.

Anyway, the corner-office set doesn't have it made. Oh, no. They grimly compete for altitude. That is, the closer to the top floor, the bigger shot you are. Top-floor folks are top dogs in the physical as well as organi-zational sense, and you'd better believe they have high-pile carpeting that's a Stainmaster version of the Serengeti Plain and covers almost as many square miles. All of us know who really does the work, though, don't we?

Jockeying for position isn't peculiar to just the cor-porate scene, however. One contractor we know confirmed that the top floors of his newly completed medical building were filled almost overnight by doctors with well-established practices. The ground floor filled last because nobody wanted to be low person on this medicinal totem pole. Its residents, newly minted M.D.s, were willing to swallow their pride temporarily.

Status and Power

Office politics revolve around status and power. Getting it, keeping it, and keeping others from getting it. They're the yin and yang of organizational politics, and they feed on each other like a chain reaction. The more you have, the more you want. The more you get, the more secure your job tends to be. At least, until

(1) Your company is gobbled up in a merger and you're demoted to picking up litter in the parking lot.
(2) Your division is liquidated because the company president needs the funds to make a "major capital investment" (new private yacht or helicopter).
(3) Your boss is replaced with an outsider who's an even more adept politician than you (an unlikely occurrence, since you were smart enough to buy this book).

If you're looking for some mind-boggling status symbols, it shouldn't take long to find them. Executives who breathe the rarified air of CEO country have toys that are excellent examples of status carried to insanely extravagant limits, which is one reason you shouldn't be the least bit self-conscious about carrying it there yourself.

For example, one CEO had an elaborate fountain built outside his window at corporate headquarters. Its pumps, nozzles, assorted spray patterns, and multicolored lights made a display that would rival most Chinese New Year's celebrations. On his desk was a panel of buttons, which he pushed to make the fountain do its tricks to amuse visiting CEOs who no doubt worked as diligently as he to convince themselves they were really earning their seven-figure salaries. (You bet they were.) Picture him, if you will, whiling away the lonely hours at the top by diddling with a gimmick that probably decreased stockholders' dividends by 50 cents per share in the year it was built.

And how about the self-effacing CEO whose company was headquartered in a New York skyscraper? He had a contractor tunnel up through several top floors (which housed climate-control equipment) to the roof to build a chimney for the wood-burning fireplace he had installed in his office. The expense was justified by the unarguable logic that a wood-burning fireplace would look real neat in his office. Who says that big companies don't support capital expenditures with detailed analyses and objective, hard-headed thinking? You can just imagine him up on the roof, a veritable Paul Bunyan in a $1,500 suit, hewing mightily at Honduras mahogany logs while he contemplates administering, delegating, controlling, and lots of other management stuff beyond the ken of us mere mortals. If you've ever wondered why the prices of some companies' products are so high, now you know part of the answer. Maybe we ought to lighten up a little on the Japanese.

We'll come back to the subject of status symbols—

and how you can accumulate some of your very own – momentarily, after we explore . . .

The Nature of Political Systems

Political systems are minigovernments whose members (politicians) seek or hold seats of power. Politicians, whether in companies or government, are sometimes known to seek personal gain, just like

- The sun sometimes rises in the east.
- The Pope is sometimes Catholic.
- The bill for auto repairs is sometimes less than the mechanic's estimate.

Corporate Culture

A company's political system exists inside its corporate culture, just like a moth exists within a cocoon. You remember what cultures do from biology class: They grow mold. As a bluffer, however, you should analyze how compatible you are with your company's unique, home-grown, in-house strain of mold. Is it hairy or smooth? Green or gray? Wet or dry? Stagnant or growing faster than the slimy creature in *Alien?* Cultural norms are the reason employees at some companies interact with all the pomp and ceremony of a diplomatic reception, while at others they display the courtesy and polish of drywall hangers.

Go to work in the wrong corporate culture, and you'll have about as much chance of survival as a possum on the freeway at rush hour. One cardinal rule of politics, then, is to avoid organizations that you can't or don't want to fit into. Here are some cheerful little examples from Real World 101:

- The president of a major cereal company had his flight on the corporate jet cut short by the chairman and CEO, who ordered it to land at a jerkwater airport. The president was summoned to a dingy room in the terminal and fired on the spot. Despite his great track record with a foreign subsidiary, his management style and personality traits rubbed the home office people the wrong way.
- Another executive, upon wheeling his foreign car into the reserved parking lot on his first day with his new employer, was disturbed to find that all his contemporaries drove domestic automobiles. Moreover, it turned out that they were extremely suspicious of anyone who didn't "Buy American." This and other aspects of the company's corporate culture made him feel as out of place as a banjo player in a symphony orchestra. He finally quit to join another firm with a more compatible culture, where he built a stellar reputation for himself.

The message, then, is this: Test the water first; look before you leap; and pick your company with its corporate culture in mind. Corporate culture clashes create a great market for bumper stickers like "A bad day fishing (at the beach, drinking to excess, in a coma, clipping your toenails) is better than a good day at work."

YOUR PLAN OF ATTACK

Scouting the Terrain

Assuming that you and your corporate culture are compatible, how do you get to know the lay of the land? It's surely not by studying the Employee Handbook and memorizing the company's code of ethics. No way.

Look instead for what's been called the "hidden hierarchy," which consists of channels of communication and certain informal movers and shakers who really make things happen. How do you do uncover this subterranean society? By asking such practical questions as

- Which coffee lounge/cafeteria table/lunch spot/ after-hours watering hole attracts the people who really know what's going on in this outfit?
- Which rules can be broken? Which can be bent, and how far?
- Which managers are respected the most? Which ones are merely tolerated?
- How and where can I tap into the most accurate branches of the grapevine?
- Which lower-level people—especially secretaries— have the most influence?
- Which pet peeves, prejudices, quirks, rituals, and

blind spots do key managers have? How can I manipulate these to my advantage?

- What recreational activities/weekend hobbies/company-sponsored sports teams are popular at this company? Which ones do my most knowledgeable or influential coworkers belong to?

Obviously, these aren't questions that you should raise your hand and put forth during the new employee orientation session – unless you're under the influence of controlled substances or a staunch believer in the Tooth Fairy. And you won't find the answers written down anywhere, either. Not even in that universal communications device, the Employee Handbook. Employee Handbooks are useless to bluffer-politicians (and to most other thinking people, for that matter) because they tell you only what the company wants you to know. What you *need* to know and what you *ought* to know aren't mentioned anywhere. Officially, that is.

Nope, you'll have to learn the rhythm and soul of the company by launching your own intelligence-gathering campaign. Introduce yourself to coworkers who seem to be informal leaders and gatekeepers of information. Be assertive and confident, but not pushy or overly enthusiastic. Volunteer discreetly for assignments that will bring you closer to people in seats of power. Insinuate yourself discreetly and diplomatically into the communications loop of those who are in the know. Listen more than you talk, and don't repeat gossip. Store it, sort it, and file away the useful stuff for future reference, but don't pass it on. The stronger your reputation for keeping confidences, the more people will confide in you — and the more you learn about what's really going on. It's as simple as that.

Informal Power

Informal power, a major part of the corporate political scene, is acquired through traded favors, charisma (which, to be honest, you either have or you don't), nepotism, or your ability to grant or withhold subtle rewards. It's as universal in today's corporate arena as designer briefcases, cellular phones, the Gold Card, and two-hour lunches.

Consider, for example, the bottom-rung foreman whose brother-in-law was plant manager. We're talkin' major-league informal power here. Anyone who was dumb enough to cross this foreman, a cum laude graduate of the Rambo School of Human Relations, was cordially informed, "I'll tell the fat man [his portly brother-in-law] on you!" The foreman's worklife was as tranquil as the eye of a hurricane, but you know what goes on outside one of those, right?

Another form of informal power, a second cousin to nepotism, is wielded by certain secretaries. Oh, they rank no higher than other secretaries as far as pay and titles go, but that doesn't matter. What matters is, they have the ear of certain VIBs (Very Influential Bosses), so get to know who these secretaries are. When they talk, listen — courteously. If they complain about you, get your resume up to date. And if they speak well of you, their bosses may be impressed. So ingratiate yourself with these powers-behind-the-throne, trying hard not to slobber on their shoes. Make sure they know who you are; be polite; say hello; make eye contact; offer tasteful compliments when the opportunity arises. Consider this an investment in your future.

Decision Making

It's an unfortunate fact of company life that you'll have to make decisions. This is never fun, but good decisions can catapult you from the outhouse to the penthouse if things work out well. Always remember, though, that corporate penthouses come equipped with trap doors. A really catastrophic decision may find you plying your executive skills in a challenging, rewarding career as Assistant to the Associate Janitor at the nearest fast-food restaurant faster than you can say, "Gimme a Big Mac and a large fries to go."

Okay, you have to make decisions. Accept that. But what rules should bluffers follow when they do? For every major decision (what "major" means is up to you), anticipate the expectations, whims, quirks, and egos of superiors, subordinates, and peers. Equally important, make sure to take advantage of everybody who benefits from your decision. They'd do the same to you. You'd better believe it.

Superiors' Reactions

Major decisions usually end up being announced in some report. This gives you an opportunity to play travel agent and send your superiors on an ego trip. Acknowledge their wisdom, guidance, support, and input. Deep down, you might believe they have the intelligence of an amoeba, but that's beside the point. Show respect for their busy schedule by placing the nuts and bolts of your decision in an executive summary at the front of the report. As for the rest of it, use your own judgment. It can be blank pages or a copy of your old college term paper on the mating habits of aardvarks, for that matter. Nobody'll notice because they'll all read the executive summary. If anything.

Cover your backside on decisions by filling the executive summary with plenty of weasel-worded phrases like "based on available information," "if current market conditions hold," or "as long as our competitive position remains stable." If your decision turns out to be a bummer, you can bluff your way out by saying "vital information wasn't available/current market conditions didn't hold/our competitive position didn't remain stable." This ploy is a mainstay of football, wherein the coach tells pregame fans, "We might win, but we could lose, and if we lose, well, I told you we might." No matter what happens, your defense is as seamless as an egg.

Subordinates' Reactions

Reports that announce your decisions should acknowledge subordinates vaguely enough to pacify them without giving them much credit. Praise their input, contributions, sacrifices (human or animal), and many hours of hard work (which may have been offset by twice as many hours of screwing off). Credit them with providing information, but *not* with interpreting it. You should take credit for that. If your decision proves to be sound, you'll get most of the glory. If it backfires, you can blame your minions for feeding you the lousy information on which your decision was based. Then, since sewage runs downhill, you can fire them to pacify higher management. Make sure to blame your predecessor (who has died, retired, or moved on) for hiring such a bunch of mental midgets in the first place.

Peers' Reactions

Your peers will probably be terrified that you'll come up with better decisions than theirs, which would lead to your getting promoted over them and paying them back for all the political garbage they've heaped on you over the past several years. You'll probably do exactly that, of course, if given the opportunity, but you'd rather not have them think so.

Anyway, because the Payback Express runs in both directions, your report should confirm your attempt to employ "teamwork" (one of the hotter buzzwords today) and use the word "empower" several dozen times on the first page alone. You should also cite repeated efforts to "touch base," "coordinate," "solicit feedback," and "obtain input," actions that imply you involved your peers to the hilt. Actually, you did whatever you wanted to, and to hell with them. It wasn't your fault they weren't in when you called their offices at 1:30 A.M. on three consecutive Sundays. Your conscience is clear.

Who Will Benefit

This is a vital political concern for bluffers because you want everybody who benefits from your decisions to be obligated to you up until, and preferably after, the day of their funeral. It worked for the Godfather; it'll work for you. Consider the following conversation:

You: Jean, I think you might be a good choice to head up the Department of Redundancy Department. I've been asked to give the board a decision by next Wednesday.

Jean: Gee, that's terrific! What an opportunity! With three kids in college and my in-laws living with us, that salary increase will really mean a lot! But hey ... you said, "might be." Is there a problem?

You: Only with transportation.

Jean: Transportation? What transportation?

You: *My* transportation. Do you think you could manage to drop by with a new BMW before the weekend? A red one would be nice. Just leave the owner's name blank on the title.

Reciprocity, like magnetism, is a powerful force with predictable results. Good bluffers put it to good use.

Image Versus Reality

Ever count how many times the word "image" appears in today's business magazines? Several thousand, at least. And that's just on the cover.

This tells you how preoccupied some people and companies are with distorting reality. Images, as any photographer will tell you, surely aren't real. They *represent* what's real; they reflect it; but they sure as hell aren't it. In business, as in other fields, people tend to confuse images with realities, and they're sometimes susceptible to accepting the image for the real thing. Politicians of every stripe *really* cash in on that tendency.

If you have trouble appreciating the difference between images and reality, try taking a photograph of Kathleen Turner or Mel Gibson to dinner sometime. A cheap date for sure, but not much fun to kiss goodnight. Or whatever.

We all play head games to change or reinforce the image that others have of us. That's standard procedure when you're trying to bluff your way in anything, from office politics to brain surgery. For your gullible business colleagues (let's call them "bluffees"), the sleight-of-hand needed to replace reality with imagery often works. For you, the bluffer, remember to guard against being carried away with someone else's bluff. Be a skeptic, the kind of person who goes backstage after the magic show to check out the props. You'll be glad you did.

There's a little principle that applies here. Call it the Bluffer's Principle of Deception. Nobody knows what you've really got in mind except you. Follow that rule, and you'll elevate bluffing to an art form and find that it applies to every activity from office politics to poker. Knowing that bluffees can't read your mind, feel free to project whatever image you choose, comfortable in the knowledge that only you know what's going on inside your head.

Major Political Strategies

Now let's examine several tried and true political strategies that seasoned and novice bluffers alike can use to project the illusion of being influential, successful, powerful, competent, dedicated, civic-minded, larger-than-life, Renaissance men or women wherever and with whomever they work.

Strategy Number One

Acquiring and Using Status Symbols (or, Affectations That Cause Sensations). This is an all-time favorite tactic of office politicians, a veritable nuclear warhead in any bluffer's arsenal. The right status symbols, strategically employed, will generate lots of beneficial gossip about your intellectual prowess, informal clout, dedication, and legendary management acumen while holding your competitors at bay.

Office Furniture

Many of us jump to conclusions about people from their material possessions: the kind of car they drive, the size and decor of their home, their neighborhood, and so forth. At work, all of these outward trappings that bespeak status, power, and success can be consolidated within the four walls of your office.

Office furniture communicates volumes about whoever spends one-third of his or her life there. It can make a powerful statement about who you are, what you are, and where you're heading.

One excellent tactic is to get yourself a gigantic desk, one with a top that's slightly smaller than the flight deck of an aircraft carrier. A desk so enormous that baby cockroaches can learn to fly by practicing touch-and-go landings on it. Complement this with a credenza or two, a coffee table (preferably with inlaid wood), and a matched set of bookcases so tall that clouds form around the top shelves under certain atmospheric conditions. Only someone with the common sense of a paperweight would try to con the number-crunchers in Accounting or Purchasing to actually buy this stuff with company bucks, of course. No way. But there's nothing to keep you from paying for it yourself. Think of it as props in the theater where you'll project your Executive Image, okay? With any luck, your accountant can probably find a way to write off the whole shebang as a business expense on your income tax.

Anyway, once purchased, you can move it into your office over the weekend. We suggest this only because you would attract too much attention by having it delivered and moved in during working hours. Especially since it might be five times more expensive than anybody else's below the vice-presidential level. The moving part shouldn't be too much trouble or expense thanks to U-Haul and your brother-in-law Vinnie. Just budget for plenty of fluids – gas for the U-Haul and a case of Old Milwaukee for Vinnie.

How should you defend such a display of opulence and ostentatiousness? Very earnestly and with unassailable logic. Use words like "productivity," "efficiency," and "access" a lot. Declare that the bookcases are for your own personal reference library (more on that later) and the desk must be large enough to hold your personal portable PC, your company-supplied PC and fax machine, your scale model of the corporate headquarters building, and your marble busts of Donald Trump, Socrates, Shakespeare, and anything else that conveys the impression that you're a loyal, dedicated, philosophical, progressive, dynamic, state-of-the-art executive. Not to mention bluffer.

If that's not enough, you can also claim you're allergic to Formica and steel, which is what company-supplied office furniture is made from. At least for people at your level. It's written into the policy manual somewhere. But there's nothing that says you can't outfit yourself at your own expense and for the perfectly legitimate reasons cited here. And so you have. Spectacularly.

Your colleagues naturally can't help but notice that your office is furnished on a scale slightly grander than that of Lee Iacocca. You can advance your illusion of power (and their paranoia) one step further by purchasing an engraved metal nameplate for each item. It can solemnly declare, "This (item of furniture) was custom built for (your name)." Attach it in a discreetly visible place so that visitors are sure to see it.

Office Accessories

Along with this extravagant furniture, consider furnishing your niche in the corporate wall with lamps that have heavy, expensive-looking brass bases and weigh about 50 pounds or so. Fill them with concrete if necessary. You can probably find some at your friendly Wal-Mart, but from a distance they literally reek of power. Especially to your coworkers, who may labor beneath factory lamps that have bare bulbs and green metal shades.

Carpeting, another accessory that complements your furniture, should not be overlooked. You can pick up some cheap at a used-carpet store. "The deeper the pile, the bigger the wheel" is a good rule of thumb. Some executives attach enormous prestige to carpeting, even to the point of measuring the height of each other's pile.

Don't overlook the impact of hanging plants, either. They're more popular in some companies than others.

If yours is one of them, feel free to decorate your office like a historical re-creation of the Hanging Gardens of Babylon. This should help your reputation to take root and blossom, thereby enabling you to stalk that big promotion more effectively. (A little botanical humor there.) One manager confided to her best friend that she wanted her office to look "like a Tarzan movie set." Once again, you may have to take the initiative (after hours or on weekends, whenever Vinnie's free) to install as much foliage as you care to. Never mind that top managers have gnomes who come by every day to water their plants, remove dead leaves, and croon old Tony Bennett songs to make them feel nurtured and loved. You can do that yourself, but lock your door first so passersby won't catch you being your own corporate gardener. Let them think that you rate visits from the company's resident Plant Fairy too. And so you must know somebody in High Places. The aura of prestige and influence created by these plants, coupled with your almost-genuine brass lamps, carpeting, and overwhelming office furniture will make a 40-megaton statement about your presence and presumed influence in the organization. Those who look influential often become so — if only by default.

Office accessories shouldn't be confined to things that are bigger than a bread box, however. Placing an assortment of odd and totally unrelated items throughout the room adds an aura of mystery to your background that will confound even the most determined attempts to figure out what makes you tick. Some examples:

- 1936 Oldsmobile door handle
- Railroad spike
- Rust-encrusted cannonball

- Antique brass padlock
- Gigantic fossilized shark's tooth
- Dummy hand grenade
- Antique inkwell
- Lug nut from Peterbilt truck
- Brick from the original corporate headquarters building (never mind that it was built out of wood)

One concluding thought about office furnishings is to cultivate a friend or two in the facilities and maintenance department. You never know who might be able to do you some good, and this will save you some of the cost of paying for all the stuff yourself. Maybe Fred, the guy in the warehouse, can pick up a cast-off piece of luxury furniture or carpeting when one of the higher-ups decides to redecorate his or her office to resemble the Taj Mahal. Every newly promoted or incoming executive does that. Rely on it. Their lawyers negotiate the clause into their employment contracts. You might be able to wangle some of their discards by depositing a few bucks or a case of Old Skullbuster in Fred's sweaty palms. Anything that you get this way is sure to eclipse your present stuff which, unless we miss our guess, is likely to be

(1) Government gray (acquired from a Pentagon garage sale),
(2) Orange crates (with the labels still attached),
(3) Boards and cinderblock (left over from your college days), or
(4) Early Salvation Army Thrift Shop

Trading up on office furniture, even if you have to do it yourself, will bring you a degree of status and clout that your contemporaries don't have. Not that they couldn't; they just didn't take the initiative like you did.

Strategy Number Two

You Are What You Read (More or Less). You're certain to have hyperobservant visitors who will notice the finer details of your office, perhaps even going so far as to measure the height of the aforementioned carpet pile. That's great. For the benefit of these nit-pickers (many of whom probably work in Accounting), you should buy or borrow several copies of *Mensa* magazine and place them strategically under the papers on your desk. Allow the title to peek out just far enough to be visible. Better yet, buy your own subscription and have it sent to your business address. That way everyone from the elves in the mail room to the secretaries in your work group will jump to the conclusion that your IQ is probably higher than the gross national product of some Third-World countries. There's nothing like implied mental horsepower to enhance your political clout.

Your apparent interests should reach far beyond *Mensa,* however. For example, there's a whole range of computer software that bespeaks power and status, and while this isn't technically reading matter, you should keep the manuals in plain sight and within easy reach on your bookshelves. Some of the most popular ones are

- *Lotus 1-2-3*
- *Symphony*
- *dBase III*
- *Harvard Project Manager*

- *ThinkTank*
- *Flight Simulator*

Remember that you don't actually have to *use* this stuff. You only have to convey the impression that you do, and that should register around 9.2 or so on the Richter scale with rivals who see the manuals lined up beside your desk. Just be sure to take their plastic shrink-wrap off them first, okay?

In addition to the above, you should accumulate an office library that implies a mind-numbing range of interests, skills, and abilities. Something on the order of Einstein or Stephen Hawking. You can do that by buying (at garage sales, flea markets, and library clearance sales) all of the following and bringing them to your office over the weekend:

- *Plutarch's Lives*
- *Bartlett's Familiar Quotations*
- The Bible
- Any biography of Howard Hughes
- *Iacocca*
- *Jane's Fighting Ships*
- *Mein Kampf*
- *Survive Safely Anywhere: The SAS Survival Manual*
- *Think and Grow Rich*
- *Running MS-DOS*
- *The Soul of a New Machine*
- Assorted novels by Ernest Hemingway
- Any management textbook written by Peter F. Drucker
- *In Search of Excellence*

. . . and at least one book on each of the following subjects:

- Primitive funeral customs
- Restoring antique automobiles, warplanes, loco-motives, jukeboxes, or houses
- Any book with a foreign language title on the spine (preferably Arabic, Chinese, or some other language that coworkers probably can't interpret)
- A technical manual on personal computer trouble-shooting and repair
- Gourmet cooking
- Investing in the stock market, real estate, and antiques
- Arbitrage
- Famous and not-so-famous gunfighters of the Old West
- Nuclear fission

Strategy Number Three

Let No Certificate Go Unhung. Certificates communicate an enormous amount of implied information about your achievements, generosity, civic-mindedness, dedication, professional commitment, and creativity. The creativity part is especially important here because you can use it to invent organizations that don't even exist and use them to honor a very special person who's particularly dear to your heart—you.

Even a commendation for your donation to the Widow of the Unknown Soldier looks credible if it's attractively framed and hung on your office wall. But beyond the documents that you've honestly earned (ignoring your certificate for being ninth grade Home Room Representative and the speeding ticket you got for doing 90 miles an hour on the way to a Grateful Dead concert), it doesn't hurt to produce a few of your own. Put differently, you shouldn't overlook your (ahem) freedom of the press. It works like this.

A good PC and a graphics program can crank out enough certificates of merit (participation, achievement, accomplishment, completion, etc.) to fill a Greyhound bus. You're limited only by your ingenuity and creative writing skill.

Said graphics program can do a marvelous job of creating impressive-looking credentials that will look patently authentic, especially if done on a laser printer. You can dream up literally dozens of official-sounding organizations, all of which conferred some honor upon you. Here are a few for starters. They aren't listed alphabetically because we're making them up as we go along. Our apologies to any that might really exist.

- Society for the Advancement of Administrative Theory
- Executive Achievement Institute
- American Association of Delegators
- American Delegation of Associators
- Quantitative Management Institute
- Association for Administrative Achievement
- International Consortium for Executive Development
- Society for the Advancement of Executive Productivity
- Management Effectiveness Institute
- Vanguard Institute for Executive Achievement
- Society for the Advancement of Administrative Technology
- Quantitative Decision-Making Society
- Network of International Administrators
- Consortium for Administrative Leadership

- Distinguished Leadership Institute
- Executive Insight Institute
- Executives For World Peace in Our Century
- Cross-Functional Confederation of Private-Sector Leadership Development Executives (North American Chapter)

Even the most humble piece of typewriter paper becomes an eye-catching badge of distinction when it's computer-printed with a fancy border like a stock certificate and lots of Olde English lettering. Feel free to confer upon yourself the accolades of your choice simply by keying them in and hitting the "print" button. Papering your office walls with lots of bogus certificates makes you look like a dynamic, foresighted, aggressive, powerful, self-sacrificing, generous, astute, progressive, involved-up-to-your-hairline executive. And that, of course, is precisely the kind of impression that bluffers in office politics want to make. You'll drive your coworkers crazy with envy and anxiety.

Strategy Number Four

A Picture's Worth a Thousand Words. The romantic and intriguing photograph ploy can blow your rivals right out of their shoes. It's meant to bluff them into believing you have a lifestyle that equals, if not exceeds, that of the rich and famous. Here are a few photo ideas for starters, along with some suggestions on where you can find them. No doubt you'll think of many more.

- A Donzi or Excalibur ocean-racing powerboat going full tilt off Miami Beach (write to either company's PR department)

- A stretch of virgin beachfront (see your travel agent)
- An aerial photograph taken during a hot-air balloon race (try *Forbes* magazine — the late Malcolm Forbes was a balloon racing fan)
- One of yourself wearing a helmet and goggles and leaning proprietarily against the cowling of a restored WWII P-51 Mustang (can be taken at any air show)
- The Taj Mahal (India Bureau of Tourism)
- The original company headquarters (your company's archives or PR Department)
- Assorted photographs of captains of industry and hot celebrities

The last you can obtain with almost no trouble at all. Simply write to company PR departments, movie studios, fan clubs, or stock photo houses and ask for them. Be sure to select a good mix of both sexes and assorted ethnic backgrounds, including Eskimo and Aborigine. Once you've got them, have a friend write highly personal messages on each photo and sign the celeb's name. Who would know what their real handwriting looks like, anyway? Some really fun personal messages would be

- Same time next year?
- You taught me all I know.
- To a born leader, from one of his/her avid followers.
- Next time it's my turn!
- To the quintessential Renaissance Person.
- With deepest gratitude for your advice on the _____ deal. I owe you one!
- Your secret's safe with me!

- To a man/woman of boundless wisdom. My deepest respect and gratitude.
- We really gave it hell, didn't we?
- To my closest sorority sister/fraternity brother during some of the best years of our lives. Yours in the bond,
- I won't tell if you won't! All the best,

Can you imagine the conclusions people will jump to when they read that stuff? You may have to charge admission to your office!

Strategy Number Five

Personal Jewelry. Personal jewelry conveys a discreet impression of clout and affluence. For example, a sort-of Rolex watch (really a Taiwan knockoff) is virtually standard equipment for bluffer-politicians of either sex. You can probably buy one for about $29.95 at your friendly weekend flea market if you get there before the cops raid the place. Oh, the name on the dial may be just a *little* bit different—perhaps "Relix" or "Rollix" or even "Sherman" or "Herbert," but it's the overall appearance of the case, band, and clasp that's important. Choose one that's authentic looking enough to withstand all but the closest scrutiny. Most likely it'll come with a Georgia guarantee (30 miles or 30 minutes, whichever comes first). If you wear it military style on the underside of your wrist, you'll add to your mystique and charisma while keeping the dial away from prying eyes. The point is to give legitimate Rolex wearers the impression that you rank right up there with them and can afford the toy to prove it.

In addition to the watch, you could also pick up a knockoff of a gold Cross pen and (if you're a high-school dropout) a college class ring. The latter can be found at a local hock shop for just a fraction of its original price and a staggering discount over the cost of a legitimate college education. Try to pick one from a fairly generic public university and without Greek fraternity or sorority letters embedded in the stone, unless you're willing to learn what they mean. Otherwise you could find yourself, under interrogation from a coworker, making up nervous reminiscences about the great times you had as a brother in the bond of dear old "triangle-and-X" (which would mean Delta Chi) during your undergraduate years at the Keokuk College of Welding and Brain Surgery.

Strategy Number Six

Wardrobe. So much has been written about business attire and dressing for success that just about anything said here would be repetitive. The definitive guru on the subject, John Molloy, has written *Dress for Success* titles for men, women, and assorted higher-order mammals as well. Some general suggestions are:

Make sure that your clothes harmonize with your corporate culture. Some companies, most notably those that make computer software, have dress codes on the order of Primitive Casual, something like you'd find in a college dorm on Saturday night. Others, like the legendary IBM, expect employees to dress and act as cavalierly as a mortician with a toothache. The point is to fit in. Perhaps the best advice came from the late Malcolm S. Forbes who said, "Looking the part helps get the chance to fill it."

If you're not sure what to wear for a particular corporate event, ask. Even if it's a social one. We're familiar with an individual who once worked in management for a large manufacturing company that transferred him to a plant in a charming Appalachian community that had the cultural ambiance of a tractor-pulling contest. The residents celebrated the first day of deer season with a human sacrifice. When plant management threw their annual employees' Christmas party, he presumed it was casual. This was a party, right? Dress casually, right? Silly boy. He showed up in a sweater and slacks, while his boss, colleagues, and (to his eternal astonishment) even the *production workers* wore suits! For a Christmas party! Most of those people hadn't dressed up since the *last* Christmas party, although many of their outfits looked as if they'd been slept in every night for a year. Chagrined, he hurried home and changed into a suit, which enabled him to blend in with the rest of the crowd. Except that he was wearing shoes.

One bluffer's tip for wardrobe care is to treat your clothes with fastidious respect, which implies that you've spent lots of money on them. The best way to do this is to buy a clothes tree for your office. If the corporate culture permits you to work in your shirt (or blouse) sleeves (some of them don't), take your jacket off and place it carefully on your clothes tree each morning, buttoning the front so it won't pull out of shape. Perform this ritual in the presence of others whenever possible. It'll make them feel like inferior slobs. Especially those who cram their jackets into an empty desk drawer at the start of the day.

Strategy Number Seven

Reserved Parking. Parking is a very sensitive

political issue in most companies. Where you park denotes either who you are or who you know. In most companies an internal organization chart is nothing more than an aerial photograph of the parking lot with people's names substituted for their cars.

Sometimes the parking issue can get pretty silly. After all, the real toilers and hewers always have to hike in from the hinterlands, while the top dogs, who come in late, leave early, take two-hour lunches, and crack the whip over those poor wretches, get to park right next to the building. But who said life was fair?

Status is a relative thing, which you can see once again in the parking lot. Although middle managers may get to park in a reserved lot, they still have to trudge from their cars to the building through snow, sleet, acid rain, and various other falling objects, including distraught executives hurling themselves from the top floor because they heard that a rival in a competing firm just received a South Pacific atoll (complete with residents) as a year-end bonus. Top executives, who are allowed to park next to the building, have reserved parking places with their names on each. The pecking order here is based on who's nearest the door. If you want to have real fun some weekend, tow a rusted-out '71 Chevy with a blown engine and flat tires out there and shove it into the first space. On Monday morning the Supreme Commander (or whatever the fancy title) will throw an apoplectic fit, issue live ammunition to the security guards, and order them to shoot the perpetrator on sight.

Some companies have a special reserved space for that epitome of dedication and commitment, the Employee of the Month. This spot will likely be yours

as your prowess at political bluffing improves, but in the meantime it shows how absurd the parking issue is. Let's say the Honored One mistakenly parks in the hallowed spot just one day past the cutoff date. Security will probably impound the car and charge $10 a day for storage. All glory is fleeting.

But how can you intimidate your peers and confound your superiors with your very own reserved parking place? The un-fun truth is, you're most likely going to have to earn it by surpassing a certain salary level. You might try a shortcut, though, by cultivating a friend in the Security department who would be willing to slip you a reserved decal of your own in exchange for a few bucks or a case of booze. Or, if there's a bit of petty larceny in your soul, you could steal one off the bumper of a retiring manager's car and put it on your own. If you're lucky, nobody will catch you.

The fact that you can park closer to the building than your colleagues will certainly be a political coup, and they'll end up scratching their heads and wondering how you managed to do it, while all along you smile your pussycat smile and say modestly, "Isn't it great to work for an outfit that rewards hard work and good performance?"

Strategy Number Eight

Making Others Look up to You. This bluffer's gambit ties back to The Desk That Ate Cleveland, which you may have bought with your own money. Most desks, you'll notice, are firmly planted on the floor. So much for tradition. If you want to give the impression of ruthless, raw, take-no-prisoners power, however, you can elevate your desk several inches *above* the floor. Don't use bricks, cinder blocks, or even old copies of the *Wall Street Journal* (all too crude). Instead, build (or hire Vinnie to build) a carpeted platform several inches high that will span the entire end of your office where your desk and chair are located, and place them on that. Now you're cooking! People who enter your office will get the impression, as you gaze magisterially down at them, that they ought to tug at their forelocks and ask your permission to speak—even if they're subcontractors who've come to fix the Xerox machine. The result, however, is that you've literally placed yourself a notch above your peers. You can amuse yourself after each meeting by bestowing benedictions on those who attended.

Defend your political platform (pun intended) by declaring that

(1) The higher altitude helps keep your sinuses clear.
(2) The change in perspective stimulates your creativity.
(3) The exercise of stepping up and down off the platform keeps you in good shape for racquetball and tennis.
(4) You use the space underneath for long-term document storage, which is cheaper than wasting company funds on additional filing cabinets.
(5) You're going to install a multimillion-dollar Cray supercomputer at your own expense, and the air conditioning ducts will run beneath the floor.

Strategy Number Nine

Use Your Car to Drive Home Your Image. Whether you drive a top-of-the-line foreign model that comes with its own mechanic in the trunk, a 4×4 jacked up high enough to clear small trees and buildings, or an aging and funky Rolls Canardly (Rolls down one hill; Canardly get up the next), the vehicle that carries you back and forth to work—and especially what's inside it—can do a lot for your image.

The things associated with your car, like those in your office, should be selected to confound, confuse, and bewilder colleagues that you take to lunch, pick up at the airport, drive to conventions, etc. Volunteer your driving services a lot—say five or six times a day—to get maximum mileage (pun intended) from all of this. Sure beats sitting behind a desk all day. Unless your car's air conditioning conks out.

Scatter an assortment of items in the glove box, in the back seat, and on the floor that, while having no conceivable bearing on your work, can promote rumors of legendary proportions about your lifestyle, thought processes, and personality. For starters, try

- Audiocassettes of AC-DC, The Beach Boys, Mozart, The Kingston Trio, Carly Simon, and Willie Nelson
- Several printed circuit boards from junked PCs or other electronic equipment
- A media guide for a nationally ranked football team such as the Florida State Seminoles
- A complete set of motivational tapes by Napoleon Hill, Earl Nightingale, or Dale Carnegie
- Several foreign-language copies of the *Wall Street Journal*
- A map of the London subway system
- A front bumper tag with your initials in nautical flags, a Pennsylvania Dutch hex symbol, the name

of an exotic Caribbean yacht charter service, or "Smile if you've had some lately" (in Latin)

If observers comment on this eclectic collage, just smile inscrutably and say something intriguing such as

- "I do some of my best thinking on the road."
- "It stimulates my creativity."
- "I've been doing a little tinkering, but my patent attorney told me not to discuss it."
- "Oh, that? It's inspiration for my work on the _____ project."
- "You should see what's in the trunk."
- "Don't look under the seat!"

THE POLITICS OF DEALING WITH PEOPLE

Hiring the Best People (Godfather Style)

As far as you're concerned, hiring the best people means hiring a stable of flunkies who would throw themselves in front of a Peterbilt if you forgot to say "Good morning" to them and will cheerfully work nights, weekends, and overtime without compensation. And that's just to wash and wax your car.

You can ensure your longevity as a political bluffer (and also as an employee) by hiring folks who can do *their* jobs adequately but don't want to take over *yours*. One tried and true technique that usually works is to remind them occasionally—say, fifteen or twenty times a day—that they just happen to owe you for everything but the air they breathe, and failure to display doglike devotion to you could cause them to lose their homes, miscellaneous vehicles, ergonomically equipped offices, and company benefits. Their families would be reduced to living in Army surplus pup tents and eating multilegged creepy-crawlies instead of porterhouse steak.

You can point out these simple realities cordially, however. Let's not be too crude. For example, when you hand out the checks each payday you should smile benignly and say things like "Guess you'll be able to keep Stephanie and Mike in college for another month, huh, Pete? Gosh, it seems like only yesterday that I decided to give you your job here." Or "How many years until the mortgage is paid off, Mary? Twenty-six or twenty-seven? Gee, that's a *long* time, isn't it? Aren't you glad I hired you?" These pleasant, personal exchanges, which are recommended by virtually every management consultant, reveal that you have the Common Touch and treat your employees as sensitive, feeling human beings whose careers hang by a thread – and guess who's holding the scissors. You'll know you've got them where you want them when they lick your hand, sit up and beg, and go bounding off to fetch you a copy of the *Wall Street Journal* before you even get out of your car in the morning.

Damning with Faint Praise

This is the verbal equivalent of giving rivals a handshake and a knife in the back at the same time. It takes a bit of coordination, but practice makes perfect! Let's say, for example, you're alone with your boss, maybe having lunch or waiting for a meeting to start. When the opportunity arises, you could say something like

- "Diana really did a thorough research job on that proposal. I'll bet we would have gotten the job, too, if she hadn't submitted the bid three days after the deadline." (Message: Diana's a screw-up who would probably be late for her own funeral.)
- "Steve's the most enthusiastic guy in the department, no doubt about it! Too bad his analysis of

the market for digital widget refinishers was so far off base, but I guess we can donate all that excess inventory to Goodwill and take a tax write-off." (Message: Steve couldn't analyze how he ties his shoes.)

- "The materials that Lee brought back from last week's conference really helped our sales forecast. I wish he hadn't missed the last day's session, but at least the hotel will drop the charges if he promises never to dive naked into the lobby fountain again." (Message: Lee should be working for a competitor—perhaps as coach of the corporate swim team.)

The point is, gosh darn it, you think these targets in your personal shooting gallery are really great people, honest you do, except for a minor flaw that makes the San Andreas fault look like a crack in the sidewalk.

Fireproofing

Fireproofing means running your own personal job security campaign, and it can be done in two ways. You can suck up to higher-ups or create your own lawyer.

Sucking up to higher-ups involves making and keeping friends in high places who may be able to save your butt if someone closer to your own level (especially your boss) embarks on a campaign to hand you your head.

The idea is to stick so close to people with genuine clout that they'll dislocate your nose if they turn a sharp corner. But how to do it? By cultivating one essential management skill, a skill that takes precedence over all others, one that is global in scope and universal in impact. That skill, of course, is playing a decent game of golf.

Once you've mastered the game (see *Bluff Your Way in Golf*), you can join assorted country clubs and company-sponsored tournaments and hang out wherever you're likely to meet—and rub shoulders with—some of your company's head honchos. By exercising poise and discretion, keeping your head down, following through, and blowing putts by just enough to let your boss's boss win the big ones, you'll soon be on a first-name basis with several folks in seats of power. Work 'em for all they're worth. Since every executive must play golf (it's a universal clause in every policy manual and part of every job description), you can be sure to meet everyone who's anyone by playing the right circuit.

But what if, like some of us, you think the game of golf is about as stupid as trying to water ski on an interstate highway? Ah, then you've got a problem, but never fear. There's a solution.

You can try the cheaper and often superior fireproofing technique of creating your own lawyer. You find a willing partner, let nature take its intercourse, produce at least one offspring, send it away to college (followed by law school), and Bingo! In just 25 years or so . . . but hey, wait a minute. What started out to be fun has gotten a little complicated. Assuming that the kid's willing and able (talk about a gamble!) to sue your boss into the poorhouse for refusing to shine your shoes on your birthday, you'll probably be within two weeks of retirement by then. Let's go for a faster and infinitely less expensive option. We call it (for lack of a better term) an "Invent-a-Lawyer" kit. It's convenient, takes up little space (being stored between your ears – no offense), and can be fashioned to suit your particular circumstances. In other words, it's your *imagination*. All you have to do is drop an occasional, discreet word or two within earshot of your boss about a very dear and close (albeit fictitious) legal eagle relative. This could be, for example, a handicapped minority female – never mind your own ethnic background – who specializes in chewing the legs off employers in wrongful discharge suits. Talk about her often – in the company cafeteria, before meetings are called to order, while having a drink after work. Chuckle at what a fire-breathing dragon she is, somebody who would make Attila the Hun look like a pioneer in urban renewal. Marvel about how she's won millions from a couple dozen *Fortune* 500 companies that she prosecuted for firing or demoting their employees illegally. You can't provide specifics, of course, because she's always claimed lawyer-client privilege when you asked about details. But details don't matter; the impression does. You want everyone who might have a hatchet to bury (in your back, that is) to know that you've got a fast gun for hire. This is a serious bluff, of course, and one that you hope will never be called. If you carry it off well, however, endowing this larger-than-life relative with the determination of a pit bulldog after a mailman should earn you the desired amount of respect and deference – aw, hell, let's call it fear – from supervisors who might otherwise do you in.

Tailgating

In a sense tailgating is supercharged fireproofing.

That is, you ingratiate yourself with an influential manager and ride his or her coattails to success. Tailgating, in other words, elevates the buddy system to an art form.

Business abounds with incidents of tailgating. For example, Michael Deaver tailgated Ronald Reagan for more than 20 years, finally ending up as Deputy Chief of Staff at the White House. Until 1987, Deaver's career had been linked to Reagan's for all of Deaver's working life.

Disciples of Robert Abboud, the head of First City Bancorp of Texas, reaped the benefits of tailgating when he hired them as subordinates after he was tapped to try to turn the troubled company around. Having been burned by organizational politics in previous corporate warfare, Abboud reportedly insists on loyalty from those close to him.

Tailgating isn't synonymous with fireproofing, however, for one main reason. If the executive whom you're tailgating makes a few catastrophic decisions or otherwise falls out of favor, guess who might be offered up as a sacrifice? Come on, now. Aha! You catch on fast. The watchword, then, is to tailgate with caution. Pick your target carefully (make sure you hitch your wagon to a rising star) and be alert for a shift in your mentor's fortunes that might result in your being converted from dedicated assistant and second-in-command to sacrificial lamb. Under the wrong circumstances, rising stars can become falling rocks.

Given the right conditions and mentor, however, it's not impossible for you to ride to near-greatness in someone else's shadow, just like sports cars can coast by tailgating an eighteen-wheeler on the interstate.

Ideally, you could accumulate a great deal of influence and informal clout merely because you're sitting at the right hand of power. But would-be tailgaters should appreciate the story of the farmer who went for his first airplane ride.

"Well, Luke, how was it?" a friend asked.

"Wonderful!" he said. "Had the time of m' life! I'd do it again in a minute. But you know," he whispered, "I never really did put m' weight down."

Tailgaters, take heed.

Empire Building for Fun and Profit

If all goes well, your bluffing strategy will expand to include a form of organizational architecture called empire building. In the spirit of Donald Trump, you'll begin to accumulate facilities, equipment, and (most important, perhaps) information that makes your department (and especially you) virtually indispensable.

Empire building's major goal is to make you appear to be not just a spoke in a wheel, but the hub itself. And since companies run on information, the best way to ensure job security and a firm political future is to control and give out lots and lots of information. It begins like this.

First, you have to identify the need for a whole bunch of reports, analyses, comparisons, summaries, and so forth that the regular DP department cannot possibly find the time to crank out. Next, volunteer *your* department to step into the breach. Make sure that everybody knows how astutely you spotted this information gap and how aggressively you moved to fill it by writing scores of memos to your boss. Send copies to all vice presidents, the CEO, the board of directors, and members of the current presidential administration in Washington. This is no time for modesty.

In order to provide this vital information, however, you must convince higher-ups to provide you with an airplane hangar full of computers, modems, and various other high-tech equipment, not to exclude your own communications satellite. You can do this, of course, with a little help from some of the higher managers that you cuddled up to earlier (see *Fireproofing*). Anyway, once you get all this stuff, it's as useless as a glass baseball bat without the proper people to run it. So you simply *must* have authorization to hire enough new people to populate a small town in North Dakota. And the more assets and people you control, the more influential you're presumed to be.

Now that you've accumulated all this equipment and a small army of people to run it, your department may be slightly crowded, to the point where some employees are subleasing their desk drawers to junior colleagues for $400 a month. So you put in a budget request for more space (after first discussing it with your boss's boss, whom you should now be playing golf with at least three times a week). No sweat. Before you know it, your department has doubled or tripled in size, employees, and facilities, and nobody in the company can pass gas without it being recorded on at least three of your regular reports.

Soon you'll discover that every department from Purchasing to Parking Lot Maintenance will be coming to you to touch base or coordinate what they plan to say in *their* reports, summaries, etc. And thus you become a prominent and thoroughly essential part of the corporate team, a vigilant gatekeeper and dispenser of information, while multiplying your salary and visibility several times over in the process. Information, properly manipulated, is knowledge, and knowledge is . . . well, you know the rest.

Long-Range Forecasting— Every Manager's Secret Weapon

Forecasting, which is about as much fun as watching bananas ripen, is also as risky as playing hopscotch in a mine field. Those are two excellent reasons why you should never do it and why you should always delegate it to some poor devil who works for you. Especially somebody who seems to have an eye on your job.

The main risk in forecasting is that you'll be wrong. In fact, you're virtually *guaranteed* to be wrong. You're trying to predict stuff that hasn't even happened yet! What all this adds up to is, if you want to sandbag pretenders to your throne, assign them some outrageous task such as predicting the market price of pork bellies next July 25th or forecasting next year's sales (plus or minus $50) for each of your company's 20 major products.

So what happens? Sooner or later (and in the above examples, you'd better believe it'll be sooner) they'll bite the big one and come up with figures so far off base that they might as well have been picked out of a hat. Maybe they were. The point is, you can now, with furrowed brow and appropriate murmured regrets, inform your victims during their annual performance reviews that they have not developed the ability to anticipate business conditions with the degree of accuracy necessary to make adequate strategic decisions in light of the current economic environment, or some such doubletalk as that. This sets the stage for your suggestion that they submit their resignation, which you have thoughtfully typed for their signature, and good luck in their new careers.

Maneuvering Your Way up the Ladder

There is no simple, by-the-numbers formula that will help you turn the typical promotional ladder into your own private express elevator. There are simply too many human factors and variables involved, and these will change, however slightly, with each change in personnel. About the only thing you can do is monitor and evaluate the circumstances and let them dictate when, how fast, and in what direction you should make your run for the roses. It's a judgment call.

With that in mind, here are some war stories that demonstrate how personal contacts, influence, and persuasion can sometimes be at least as important as ability and performance. Perhaps the only thing these coups have in common is that the executives who pulled them off were adept at scouting the terrain, assessing their relative power, and acting boldly and decisively when the opportunity presented itself. In other words, they were master strategists of office politics and, in some cases, quintessential SOBs.

The departing chairman and CEO of one large food conglomerate established what he thought was a solid line of succession by anointing one of his faithful subordinates, 45-year-old Executive A, as chairman and 62-year-old Executive B as president and CEO. The outgoing manager believed that Executive B, who would reach mandatory retirement age in three years, would relinquish all the marbles to his younger colleague then. Oh yeah? Cunning Executive B, who knew where lots of bodies were buried and had worked most of his career to become head honcho, persuaded directors to amend the company's mandatory retirement rule so he could hold down the top job far longer than anyone anticipated. In addition, he purged the corporation of anyone who was closely allied with the departed CEO, including, of course, his potential successor, youthful Executive A. This maneuver underscores not only the value of political savvy but also the irrelevance of education. Executive B had only a high school diploma and started his career hauling ice for refrigerated railroad cars. The other two guys were both law school graduates. As one battle-scarred old warhorse put it, "Age and treachery can beat youth and ambition anytime."

In the early days of his career, one of the country's best-known media executives worked as a reporter for a large metropolitan newspaper. When told of his first big promotion, he asked his boss to postpone it so he could spend time in several departments and learn more about the paper's operations. His coworkers, thinking that he was just one of the guys, spilled their guts to him as he worked his way through the newsroom. The grass-roots intelligence that he gathered from his "peers" proved very valuable when he moved on up the ladder. Some years later, after reaching top management at another company, he convinced the chairman and CEO to make him president. With that title under his belt, he then persuaded outside directors to make him CEO as well, thus grabbing even more power from the manager who had helped him to become president in the first place. Said he, "I believe in practicing the SOB's Golden Rule: 'Expect others to do unto you what you would do to them.'"

An obscure middle manager who needed a ride back to his hotel from a convention was offered a lift by one of his company's vice presidents. The VP, who had several drinks too many, was stopped for drunk driving. As luck would have it (and by now you should appreciate that luck can have a lot to do with success), the junior executive's cousin just happened to be the chief of police. No charges were filed against the VP, and the incident was not recorded in the police log. Several months later the junior executive received a promotion that doubled his salary. It's nice to do favors for those who know how to say thanks.

THE POLITICS OF SEPARATION

"Separation" is just a fancy word applied to people who quit or were fired or laid off. Because your path may cross with theirs again someday, you might have to be on reasonably good terms with them. Especially if they outrank you then.

LIAR Lines

Here we'd like to defer to Professor Robert Thornton of Lehigh University, who has produced a Lexicon of Inconspicuously Ambiguous Recommendations—"LIAR Lines." If departing employees or coworkers ask you for a recommendation, you can confidently use one or more of the following phrases without fear of being sued for defamation of character:

- I most enthusiastically recommend this candidate with no qualifications whatsoever.
- In my opinion, you will be very fortunate to get this person to work for you.
- I am pleased to say that this person is a former colleague of mine.
- I can assure you that no person would be better for the job.
- I would urge you to waste no time in offering this person a job.

- I cannot say enough good things about this candidate or recommend him/her too highly.

If these sound too good, read them through a second time. Sound different now?

Let a Consultant Do Your Dirty Work

This is a higher-level bluffer's tactic, but it's never too soon to learn it. After all, we're assuming that you'll climb high enough to use it sooner or later.

Assuming you have the authority, you can hire an outside consultant when you've got an especially dirty job to do. Such as shutting down half the company or axing several subordinates who are about to make a play for your job.

Perhaps the most important thing to remember about hiring a consultant is to leave no doubt who's going to authorize payment of that ridiculous $4,000-a-day fee. You are, and the consultant had better believe it. Now that that's settled, you can proceed to give him or her a neat list (preferably typewritten and double spaced) of the "findings" and "recommendations" that you want included in the summary report when the engagement is over. These should include such things as the specific positions (read "rivals") that should be dissolved and which projects should be terminated, postponed, re-evaluated, sent back for review, or otherwise torpedoed, and which subsidiaries, products, or other business segments should be liquidated no later than this coming Friday.

You realize, of course, that all hell's going to break

loose when you rubber-stamp those recommendations. What you've done, however, is make the consultant a handsomely paid scapegoat. Defend your actions by citing the consultant's academic and industrial credentials (make up a few, if necessary), as well as the staggering fee. After all, the cost must be justified, and the perfect justification is to follow the consultant's advice to the letter. You've paid a pretty penny for it, and you're determined to get your money's worth. Yeah. Sure.

THE POLITICAL SIDE OF COMMUNICATION

It's been said by somebody or other that communication is the essence of management. Whoever said that should have added that it's the essence of good bluffing too. Several communication barriers may be used to your advantage, so it's important for you to understand them and appreciate what they can do.

Inference-Observation Confusion

This is the tendency of people to jump to conclusions (draw unjustified inferences) about what they see or hear. Some of the earlier suggestions employ I-O confusion to the hilt; we just didn't attach a label to it until now.

For example, you're cashing in on I-O confusion with your office furniture and accessories mentioned earlier. Not to mention your *Mensa* magazine, computer software, weird personal library, photographs, fabricated certificates of merit, jewelry, wardrobe, and so forth. It's a short step from seeing or hearing to concluding, but some people need a little assistance. You're certainly available to help. Anything beneficial they might conclude from what they see or hear about you simply enhances your status, power, and reputation.

Bypassing

Bypassing takes advantage of the fact that words can mean anything you want them to. Because we all have our own private mental dictionaries for the words we speak and hear, adroit bluffers can often say or write one thing, while meaning the opposite. Your victim may go away feeling as happy as Dracula at sunset, without realizing what you really meant. Bypassing was the keystone of the LIAR Lines mentioned earlier, but it can be applied to any situation where you want to do a verbal tap dance.

For example, consider the case of a legislator who, upon being accused of calling one of his colleagues an ass, replied, "It is alleged that I have called my esteemed colleague an ass. This is true, and I am sorry for it."

Likewise, you might use bypassing like so:

- "Smedley, you did a hell of a job on that project last week. I've never seen performance like that before." (Smedley could be out-performed by a tree stump.)
- "Your order is off the production line. It's going through an aging process." (We've lost it somewhere in the warehouse.)
- "That's a really interesting concept, Karen!" (As interesting as a slow-motion snail race.)
- "Mark's new house is really charming." (As charming as a truck-stop restroom.)

Making Obfuscation Work for You

Every bluffer-politician should have a firm grasp of

some of the more popular and generic business euphemisms. Use them to dazzle people with your verbal footwork. Those with a high B.S. tolerance may succumb to the bluff that you're a very heavy thinker, one who operates on a plane above regular folks. Try these on for size:

WHAT YOU SAY	WHAT YOU MEAN
I'm making a survey.	I need more time to think of an answer.
Research efforts are under way.	I'm trying to find the file.
Based on our current instructions.	I don't know what they are. Do you?
According to present indications.	One wild guess is as good as another.
Use your own discretion.	Stick your neck out; see if I care.
There's a growing body of opinion.	Two managers agree.
It's a widely held opinion.	Three managers agree.
Let's meet to discuss this.	Are you as confused as I am?
This deserves program status.	It's too complicated to handle with a phone call.
This office is concerned.	Cut the crap.

Please notify this office.	If you don't keep me informed, you're history.
I am not in a position to . . .	If you think you can change my mind, you must be out of yours.
I have taken your proposal under consideration.	I'll agree to it just as soon as hell freezes over.
You've been assigned to a mobility pool for derecruitment.	You're fired.
This job is filled with challenges and opportunities.	It's loaded with headaches and problems.
Try to get me the report by Friday.	If you don't, you'll be unemployed on Monday.
This is a people-oriented company.	Our pay's lousy, but we give free turkeys at Christmas.
We're a very close-knit group.	We're understaffed, so you'd better plan to work nights and weekends.
We're launching an attitude management campaign.	We're cranking up a new PR blitz to B.S. our way out of this crisis.
That was a strategic misrepresentation.	I lied.

In addition to the above, you should cultivate the

ability to make the mundane sound profound. A gift for doublespeak (making verbal mountains out of molehills) adds gravity to your subject while amplifying its importance beyond all reason. What you don't want people to realize, of course, is the transparent simplicity of the subject you're talking or writing about. If they did, they'd probably ignore you.

But ah, the power of words. You can use the following random sample of King Kong phrases and their pedestrian ideas or objects as a guide to creating your own private doublespeak glossary, no matter what you do.

WHAT IT'S CALLED	WHAT IT MEANS
Hydroforce blast cup	Toilet plunger
Patron assistance center	Concession stand
Eligibility technician	Welfare clerk
Destination advisor	Travel agent
Revenue enhancement	Tax increase
Unlawful or arbitrary deprivation of life	Killing
Interface	Meet and talk
Home plaque-removal instrument	Toothbrush
Nutritional-avoidance therapy	Diet
Uncontrolled contact with the ground	Plane crash

Grain-consuming animal units	Chickens, pigs, and cows
Energetic disassembly	Explosion
Hexiform rotatable surface compression units	Hex nuts
Personal-protection specialist	Bodyguard
Ground-mounted confirmatory route	Road sign marker
Career alternative enhancement	Employee layoff program
Diagnostic misadventure of a high magnitude	Medical malpractice

High-Tech Bluffing

Burying Land Mines on Computer Disks

Desktop computers are as common as dirt in today's businesses, which means that an awful lot of information—some good, some bad, and some that's infinitely helpful to bluffers—can be swapped by electronic means.

The point was made earlier that you should be computer literate. It stands to reason, then, that rivals will suspect you of keeping lots of sensitive data on computer diskettes that you've hidden away as carefully as misers hide their gold.

Don't disappoint them.

Sure, you've probably got lots of sensitive stuff stored on computer diskettes, but no, you're not stupid enough to hide them in your office, or anywhere within a five-mile radius of the place. Instead, what you should "hide" in your office is several diskettes with *totally fictitious, worthless garbage* that your rivals will *believe* is valuable data. Furthermore, you should put these diskettes in a really ingenious hiding place like underneath your desk blotter or in your bookcase. You should also identify them with words that won't attract much attention. Words like "Top Secret" or "Confidential" should work just fine.

So what are you trying to do with all of this? Set a trap with electronic bait, hoping that some of your more treacherous colleagues will enter your office someday, call up the bogus data from your "secret" disks, and use it to make complete fools of themselves. Gotcha! This ploy is really nothing more than a high-tech version of the age-old military tactic of sending false information to the enemy.

What kind of data should you fabricate? Use your imagination. For starters you might try pie-in-the-sky sales forecasts, cost figures, or profit projections. A totally fictitious budget for the upcoming fiscal period might be nice. You could also save a variety of memos outlining your views about certain projects, policies, marketing plans, or whatever. Just make sure that whatever is on this diskette is precisely the opposite of your real views. You could also store notes to yourself about meetings you supposedly had with higher-ups in which they praised your decisions, guaranteed you a promotion, gave you privileged information, granted some special concessions, or did something else to demonstrate beyond a shadow of a doubt that you've got the inside track.

Personal data would be fun to work up, too. You could make up an entire spreadsheet full of fake investment data showing that you're worth several million dollars or write memos to a nonexistent financial planner outlining your ideas for investing your multi-million-dollar trust fund or lottery winnings. Whatever you decide to save, take the time to make it seem so genuine that anyone who sees it will be certain that they've really stumbled onto something.

Once you've got the disks properly formatted, labeled, and baited, set the trap by making sure that several colleagues know about them. For example, you could fumble around, drop them on the floor, pick them up, and hurriedly stuff them under your desk blotter when someone enters your office unexpectedly. Or leave them jutting out from between two books in your bookcase so you can furtively shove them back out of sight as you pace the floor during a meeting.

Your actions must be so natural that anyone with the nerve to get the disks and read or copy them will believe they've stumbled onto a mother lode. Their next step, most likely, will be to use this totally worthless information in their own reports, memos, or proposals to higher management. And since it's totally worthless, sooner or later they'll look like imbeciles. When they do, you'll know who's been rummaging through your things while you were out. A most useful piece of information, that.

Power Toys That Enhance Your Image

Okay, everybody! Checkbooks and credit cards ready? Here we go! If your budget and line of credit permit, you can stage an assault on the senses of all but the most jaundiced colleagues by laying in a supply of high-tech toys that will place you virtually in a class by yourself. The cumulative result is that others will see you as an executive version of Robocop. Some of the more impressive high-tech toys are:

Sharp Wizard electronic organizer. This doodad works on memory cards and is handy for tallying expenses, translating a foreign language, or serving as a hand-held dictionary. It costs about $299.

Ricoh MC 50 copier with fax attachment. No on-the-go manager should leave home without one. The copier weighs about three pounds and can scan and duplicate up to 4×6 inch images; the fax attachment weighs two pounds. Cost: $540 for each.

Motorola MicroTac 950 portable cellular telephone. A cellular phone is standard equipment for any self-respecting bluffer, and this one is really special. It fits in a shirt pocket, stores and displays 120 phone numbers, and weighs only 12 ounces. The cost is just a modest $249.58 per ounce ($2,995).

Reebok pump high-top basketball shoes. Just the thing to inflate your arches and your ego simultaneously before the big game with those smartasses in the purchasing department. A basketball-shaped air pump built into the tongue inflates the linings to your liking. Makes every slam dunk feel, well, as comfortable as an old shoe. Cost? Just a modest $85. Per foot.

Lotus QuoTrek portable electronic tickertape. Be the first kid in your office to call up data on up to 72 stocks, options, and futures. Then call your broker (on your Motorola MicroTac) to get in on the ground floor. Or fax him a memo on your Ricoh MC 50. No matter what, you'll jump for joy (in your Reebok pump high-tops) when your envious colleagues reveal their despair at your one-upmanship by jumping off the roof. Cost of the QuoTrek: $399 plus $63 monthly fee.

Laserex Laser Pointer. This gimmick appeals to the latent magician in every political bluffer. It can shoot a battery-powered beam of red laser light half the length of a football field in daylight or darkness. Great for humbling arrogant waiters who contract selective blindness when you're ready to call for the check. Ought to be accompanied with a death-ray amplifier so you could vaporize hecklers, rivals, and obnoxious members of the audience while you're making an important presentation. Cost: $395.

Portable PC. This was mentioned earlier as partial justification for having a desk the size of a Little League field, but some specifics are in order here. One important point is to make sure that everyone sees you carrying it into the office each morning. Link it with your office PC by modem so you can download data from one to the other.

A portable PC and a modem will allow you to work at home a lot, and that alone justifies the expense. If your boss complains about trivia such as company policy, work schedules, and showing up at the office every day, you might counter with

- "My time log shows that I'm 20 percent more productive at home! This PC lets me convert useless commuting time into valuable working hours. In fact, working at home on a PC gives the company _____ more hours of my time every week!"
- "It's the wave of the future! All *progressive* executives acknowledge the value of home-based workstations today, as I'm sure you know." (This is a

gracious way of saying, "You Cro-Magnon! Where have you been for the last decade! You're technologically obsolete and don't know it!")

- "Which do you want, quality or volume? If you want me to look busy, I'll dress up, commute for _____ hours every day, and work here. If you want productivity and efficiency, let me operate at home."

Flattery May Get You Anywhere (or at Least Give You a Head Start)

Every bluffer-politician needs to have a few flattering phrases on the tip of his or her tongue. They needn't be exaggerated, fawning, brown-nosing remarks. Not all of them, at least. But when the atmosphere calls for a gentle stroke to a higher manager's or a gullible rival's ego, consider the following:

- "If you looked up 'creativity' in the dictionary, you'd find his (her) picture!"
- "You really have a sense of style!"
- "Hey, when this guy/gal talks, I listen!"
- "You're a thinker. No wonder you've risen so fast in this company."
- "If I had your gift for _____, I'd have it made."
- "If I had your money . . ."
- "He (She) is a genius. An *absolute genius!*"

A Notable Suggestion
(but an Awful Pun)

As part of your personal routine, begin carrying a pocket-sized spiral notebook with you wherever you go, and jot down things intermittently throughout the day. Take special pains to do this around your co-workers, especially during lunch or while having an after-work drink or waiting for a meeting to start. It goes without saying that you should always write with your knockoff Cross pen, and make sure to check your so-called Rolex watch frequently, as if working under a high-pressure deadline.

Stare off into space occasionally as if summoning the muse or pondering a great unsolved mystery of the universe. Such as whether you'll be able to meet your mortgage payment this month or make it until payday without exceeding the credit line on your Visa card again. Affect a worried expression like Einstein probably did while conceiving his theory of relativity. Then raise one eyebrow, allow a wry smile to flicker across your lips (inspiration has come!), and begin to write once more.

This frequent, contemplative, cerebral bluff will do at least two things:

(1) Convince higher managers that you're a go-getter who keeps a perpetual inventory of "action items" and "significant incidents" for follow-up and future reference.

(2) Scare the crap out of peers who can't imagine what you could possibly find to write down during times when they're most likely mentally

masturbating or coasting in cerebral overdrive and hoping nobody will notice.

A word of caution, though. Don't let anyone look over your shoulder. They might see that you're only making a shopping list or working out an estimated bar bill for the month.

BON VOYAGE

Well, we're nearing the end of our little journey, and we hope you've had a pleasant trip. Please keep this handy guide nearby for ready reference as you launch your assault on your unsuspecting colleagues first thing in the morning. Just don't let them borrow it from you, okay? In fact, considering the potentially catastrophic consequences of that, maybe you should dash out right now and buy up all the remaining copies in the bookstore, just to keep them from falling into enemy hands. Go ahead. We'll wait.

There now, don't you feel better? You'll sleep well tonight knowing your rivals' careers will have all the mobility of a fire hydrant, while you can expect to see your picture on the cover of *Forbes* or *Fortune* within the next month or two. Which will mean you've earned the company of some world-class bluffers in office politics.

Fair wind and good weather be with you.

The biggest bluff about the *Bluffer's Guides* is the title. These books are full of information — and fun.

NOW IN STOCK — $3.95

Bluff Your Way in Baseball
Bluff Your Way in British Theatre
Bluff Your Way in Computers
Bluff Your Way in the Deep South
Bluff Your Way in Football
Bluff Your Way in Golf
Bluff Your Way in Gourmet Cooking
Bluff Your Way in Hollywood
Bluff Your Way in Japan

Bluff Your Way in Management
Bluff Your Way in Marketing
Bluff Your Way in Music
Bluff Your Way in New York
Bluff Your Way in the Occult
Bluff Your Way in Paris
Bluff Your Way in Public Speaking
Bluff Your Way in Wine
Bluffer's Guide to Bluffing

NEW TITLES

Bluff Your Way in the Great Outdoors
Bluff Your Way in Home Maintenance
Bluff Your Way in Math
Bluff Your Way in Office Politics
Bluff Your Way in Philosophy
Bluff Your Way in Psychology
Bluff Your Way in Sex

To order any of the Bluffer's Guides titles above,
use the order form on the next page.

AVAILABLE SOON

Bluff Your Way in Basketball
Bluff Your Way in Dining Out
Bluff Your Way in Etiquette
Bluff Your Way in Fitness
Bluff Your Way in Las Vegas
Bluff Your Way in London
Bluff Your Way in Marriage
Bluff Your Way in Parenting
Bluff Your Way in Politics
Bluff Your Way in Relationships

Get Bluffer's Guides at your bookstore or use this order form to send for the copies you want. Send it with your check or money order to:

Centennial Press
Box 82087
Lincoln, NE 68501

Title	Quantity	$3.95 Each
Total Enclosed		

Name_____

Address_____

City _____

State_____ Zip_____